POLISHED

by

FRICTION

Charleston, SC
www.PalmettoPublishing.com

Polished by Friction: A Journal

Hardcover ISBN: 979-8-8229-2770-4
Paperback ISBN: 979-8-8229-2771-1

POLISHED

by

FRICTION

BY DIVINE PURPOSE

In an effort to heal from the traumas of my past, I decided to put pen to paper. This was a challenging task; however, it was necessary for me to heal and move forward as a strong fortified woman. My story is meant to relate to individuals on a soul level. Once the soul is healed, the mind and the body will follow. I wanted to give the reader snippets of my life to help nudge them to a path of healing and freedom.

This journal takes the reader through thirty-one days in the life of the author. The reader should dedicate at least twenty-four to forty-eight hours to reading and writing. The reader can take more time if needed, as some topics may be more sensitive than others. At the end of the thirty-one days, the reader should feel lighter in their spirit and soul due to them unpacking the things that have weighed them down over the years. I would encourage the reader to find a quiet place to read, write, reflect, meditate, pray, and allow the healing to begin.

Table *of* Contents

Introduction

This journal is for anyone who has ever been hurt, ostracized, abused, mistreated, isolated, abandoned, or rejected. Journaling is a therapeutic tool that can be used to *heal* you everywhere you are carrying baggage and make room for God to have His perfect will and way in your life. Sometimes the closest ones to you will not understand how you feel, but if you put your feelings on paper, it is like relinquishing your issues to a listening ear. I implore you to take the time to really think about your feelings at the time of the issue; dig deep! As you cut away the layers of pain and the shadows of your past, God will in turn give you a reason to praise *him*. I pray that this journal gives you the strength to keep pressing and move forward.
May abundant blessings and supernatural overflow be yours!

Sincerely,
Divine Purpose

“A gem cannot be polished without friction, nor a man perfected without trials.”

—Confucius.

I was born to a fifteen-year-old mother and an eighteen-year-old father. My maternal grandmother attempted to have me aborted; however, my biological mother was too far along. To conceal the embarrassment of having a pregnant teen, my maternal grandmother told everyone that my biological mother was dying of cancer.

How horrific! Who knew that cancer made your belly large and caused significant weight gain?

After my biological mother gave birth, I was left at the hospital and placed in the system. I was considered an orphan; a ward of the state. My foster mom, who was Caucasian, said I was a good baby. I was told that she wanted to adopt me; however, interracial adoptions weren't as popular in the 1970s as they are now. Sandra Bullock, Madonna, and Angelina Jolie have popularized interracial adoption. Where were the celebs when I needed them (smile)?

I eventually found my way into the home of a couple that couldn't conceive. The husband was a Vietnam War veteran and his wife had a tilted womb—that wasn't the only thing tilted about that woman.

Growing up with this couple, I experienced many heartbreaks, deferred dreams, and devastation that no child should experience.

I recall washing my clothes in the bathtub and hanging them around the house to dry. I used to heat a pot of water on top of the kerosene heater to wash up or take a bath. The microwave oven had become my stove because they didn't purchase propane. Cereal and TV dinners were a staple in this household. Meals were never planned. We ate out on a regular basis. Diners were popular in the Tri-State area, and we were well known at two diners in the Bridgeport, Connecticut, area. Go figure.

As a child, I fantasized about what it would be like to grow up in a household where I was loved, protected, and hugged. I wanted to be accepted and treated like a princess. I watched from the sidelines as my friends were treated as the apple of their family's eye and noticed a significant difference between how they were treated and how I was treated. What was it about me that deemed me unworthy, unlovable, and unacceptable?

In my opinion, my assigned parents shouldn't have had custody of me. They weren't fit to parent anything, let alone another human being. I was abused physically, mentally, emotionally, and—down the road—sexually. I was a hefty child; very chubby! I believe all the eating out contributed to my overweight status. I couldn't wear Garanimals or the cute sets they sold at Bradlee's, because they didn't come in my size. I had to wear clothes from the Pretty Plus section at Sears. On top of being fat and overweight, I had significantly wide feet, known as Flintstone feet. It was a challenge for me to find cute shoes—this was a hard pill to swallow, especially for a girl with a serious shoe fetish. I longed to wear the cute, slinky, contoured shoes; however, the width of my feet wouldn't accommodate such taste. My assigned mother didn't make the situation any more pleasant; she often expressed her dislike of my rotund body and fat feet. She said that it was hard finding shoes and clothes to fit me. These were just some of her many complaints as it related to me.

My assigned father was a pastor and had a few jobs during my time living with them. He was a salesman for Lipton Tea, an auto mechanic at Sears, a videographer/editor, and a printer repair tech for Xerox. My assigned dad loved everything that had to do with church. I attended church all day on Sunday; Tuesday night was Bible study; Wednesday night was prayer; Friday night was worship service; and Saturday was choir rehearsal. Church was a significant part of my upbringing and I often felt it was cultish.

The church organization my assigned father was affiliated with was called the Fire Baptized Holiness Church of God of the Americas, aka the FBH movement. To be a part of this organization, you were required to follow the rules and regulations they outlined in a black book called *The Discipline*. Some of the sordid things I recall from this book of ridiculousness were as follows: No partaking in strong drinks (including Coca-Cola); women couldn't wear pants or any apparel that a male would particularly wear; women could not wear makeup; no smoking; you were allowed to get divorced—however, if your ex-spouse was not deceased, you could not remarry. Do you see the picture I am painting here? Every quarter, the elder of the district would visit a collection of storefront churches in their assigned area and collect money from the members, some of whom were of meager means. They would browbeat them to give "freewill" offerings and tithes under the pretext that God was going to return that same money they sowed into the church back to them ("good measure, pressed down, shaken together, and running over"). My assigned dad believed in this church organization so much that he would pay the church mortgage before paying his home mortgage. He felt as though this was the proper thing to do. I used to tell him that his family was his first ministry; however, my ideas fell on deaf ears, as he begged to differ.

One summer my assigned dad said that the Lord had told him to shut in the church and fast. We literally lived at the church; we ate there, slept there, etc. I was unhappy with these arrangements. While my friends were living their best young lives, I was at church praying for God to let someone call and ask if I could sleep over at their house or something. Being that we were fasting, we ate cheese, eggs, and broccoli for dinner. Looking back on this event, I shake my head, because I couldn't imagine subjecting my child to this type of living circumstance.

During this consecration/fast, one of the members' spouses got saved and accepted Christ. He later became a bishop in a leading church organization. My assigned father sacrificed our summer, finances, family time, etc. to lay before God on behalf of his flock. I understand the sacrifices of a leader; however, I often resented the church because I never had the opportunity to live a normal life outside of the confines of this religious construct that ruled every area of my existence.

The church often had fellowship days, conventions, revivals, plays, etc. that we had to participate in. I often felt like the odd kid out, because I wasn't cool enough to hang with the popular Pastor's Kids (PKs). I have always been different, felt different, and looked different. I would soon learn that different would be my normal.

Church gave me a false sense of reality—what I thought was real wasn't. I often found myself questioning the life decisions my assigned dad made based on the church's view. I didn't understand how someone with such vast formal education was so deeply indoctrinated in religion and not relationship.

Anyone who knew me knew that I got along better with my assigned father than his first wife. I dare not give her the title of mother, as it would singe the very pages of this book. My assigned father hadn't wanted to take me into their home and be responsible for my well-being. He'd been opposed to this idea because he had to help his mother raise his six siblings when his dad walked out on them. I can understand his position; however, I just wish the Department of Family and Children's Services of Westchester County had known this information prior to placing me in the care of this unfit couple.

My assigned father used to tell me that he wasn't raising me as a girl, but rather a human being. He taught me how to perform brake jobs, change spark plugs, check the tread on a tire, and drive a manual transmission automobile.

My assigned father was there but not there. He was aloof and silent when it came to the treacherous ways of discipline his wife inflicted upon me. In my opinion, his silence was an approval of sorts for how she treated me.

I recall a time in my childhood when I didn't want to live anymore. I wrote a note and went into my assigned dad's armoire and swallowed a handful of his pain meds that he'd gotten from the doctor after his orthoscopic knee surgery. I fell asleep in my room and woke up late that evening, only disappointed that I had woken up alive and not somewhere in the great beyond. I had grown weary of the abuse.

I was always a good student in all my subjects, apart from math. In the fifth grade, I won first prize for my essay on brotherhood. I read the essay in front of the entire student body at Park City Magnet North Campus and some members of the board of education—that win made me feel very accomplished.

My eighth-grade graduation was a milestone. I was appointed to pray during the opening ceremony and again for the closing. I was so proud that I was going to mount the podium in front of everyone; however, the one person I wanted to be there to hear me was absent. My assigned father was always tardy to everything outside of church events. He took pictures on his Minolta camera; however, the roll of film got stuck, and he never bothered to resolve the issue. I was let down that day. While my friends received flowers, cards, and gifts, I was there with an armful of awards and no sentiment of praise. "If your own tribe cannot celebrate you, what are we here for?" is what was going through my mind. This was one of the many voids in my life.

After my eighth-grade graduation, my clothes (summer and winter) were packed into a suitcase, and I was driven to Springfield Gardens, New York, where my assigned father's sister resided. She lived right off the Conduit/Belt Parkway. The summer of '87 was different from any other summer, because this time instead of returning home, I stayed with my assigned grandmother on my assigned father's side.

Over the course of the summer, I told my assigned grandmother of the different counts of abuse I suffered by being locked in the basement, being burned with the curling iron, receiving verbal abuse, etc. I knew I didn't want to return there, and if my assigned grandmother had anything to do with it, I wouldn't. When it was time for me to start my ninth-grade year of high school, my grandmother enrolled me in Dominican Commercial High School in Jamaica, Queens, New York. I was elated to get this fresh start.

On my first day of school, I met a young lady from Brooklyn, New York. She has been my A1 from day one. Khriscynthia Anderson has been a confidant, sister, friend, life coach, cheerleader, etc. I cherish our relationship immensely. There were times when I didn't have lunch money and she would split her lunch with me. I thank God for placing her in my life at such a young age.

During my sophomore year of high school, it was discovered that my grandmother had breast cancer—such a devastating blow. I remember going to North Shore Hospital to see her. It was painful to see her in this condition. She was my heart. During my junior year, I had to move back in with my assigned father, because my assigned grandmother's cancer was getting worse. I found out that had my assigned grandmother had the recommended mastectomy that had been offered in the early stage of her diagnosis, the possibility of the cancer metastasizing would have been less. My assigned grandmother was a pastor, prophetess, and a spiritual powerhouse. She was a praying woman. Even in her illness, she constantly gave God the glory. When she was in pain, she would yell out, "Jesus!", "Glory!", and "Hallelujah!" They don't make 'em like her anymore.

The first part of my junior year in high school was spent at a Catholic school in Connecticut. Halfway through the school year, we had to move.

The reason for the move was because the church organization my assigned father was affiliated with gave him a promotion of sorts. He was appointed to be the pastor of the founding bishop's church that was in Atlanta, Georgia. By their organizational standards, this was making it to the big time. I was not impressed.

At the time I was fifteen years old with a learner's permit. Our home in Connecticut was being foreclosed upon, and my assigned father and I had to relocate to Atlanta. I drove one car and he drove the other. Who would allow a fifteen-year-old with only a learner's permit to drive from Connecticut to New York, and then to Georgia? Only my assigned father! It was an exciting road trip, to say the least.

The latter part of my junior year was spent at a high school on the west side of Atlanta, Georgia. I had a difficult time adjusting, because I was so used to being around girls all the time. It was different attending a co-ed school. My assigned father wanted me to attend the recommended school; however, I didn't fit in there. The kids were bougie and stuck up. I had no knowledge of where they were in their studies. I was afraid that I was going to fail. One morning my assigned father woke me up for school, and I told him that I was not going if I had to continue attending that school. I locked myself in the bathroom. After an hour of yelling and screaming, he finally gave in and enrolled me in the school that was in my district. I qualified for their magnet program and finished the latter part of my junior year with flying colors. When I got out of school in May, I headed back to New York. I didn't like Georgia. All my friends were in New York and I wanted to graduate with them.

Upon arriving in New York, I stayed with one of my assigned father's sisters. On August 9, 1990, I went to visit my assigned grandmother. She was staying with one of her daughters in Queens Village. I saw her take her last breath—it was heartbreaking When the ambulance arrived, they made several attempts to resuscitate her; however, she had already transitioned. I was numb. My assigned grandmother was a precious gem, my advocate, my intercessor, and my girl. She was gone. I was devastated, to say the least.

The next morning I accompanied my assigned aunt to the funeral home. We selected a shroud and casket for the funeral. I was moving in slow motion and disbelief—this was an arduous pill to swallow. The one person who had my back 1,000 percent was gone. This wasn't only a tragedy for me but for her entire family, as she was the matriarchal glue that held everyone together in harmony.

School started in September. This was my senior year of high school; however, I was depressed. My assigned father was in Georgia pastoring the bishop's church. In the spring of 1991, my assigned father reconnected with a former girlfriend he had dated in New York prior to going off to Vietnam. Her mother was a pastor. His former girlfriend, her mother, and her mother's congregation relocated to Macon, Georgia, which is about an hour and forty-five minutes outside of Atlanta, Georgia. My assigned father proposed to her for the second time and she agreed to become his wife. According to my assigned father, he spent somewhere in the area of ten thousand dollars for her engagement ring. Fancy!

In May of 1991, I was preparing my high school graduation invitations. I proudly handed them out. I thought for certain that my assigned father's family would attend; however, nobody showed up! When I arrived at the graduation ceremony, my principal asked me to step out of line because I had an unpaid tuition balance. I was embarrassed and, quite frankly, dumbfounded. Everyone was asking me what was wrong. One of my tenth-grade teachers, Sister Rita Haberlack, came to my rescue. She told my principal that it wasn't my fault that my tuition wasn't paid. She advised that I was a good student who at least deserved to walk, because I couldn't get that moment back. I marched but was slightly angry that my assigned father had driven all the way up to New York knowing that my tuition was in arrears; I didn't understand that.

After the graduation ceremony, my assigned father's sister, with whom I was residing, started tripping about me being there. I had no concrete plans for college, even though I had received a partial scholarship to NYU! I was accepted at Tuskegee, Clark Atlanta University, St. John's University, and a few others. I had no guidance in this area. My assigned father, who held a plethora of degrees, never talked to me about my future or career aspirations. There was no plan for me.

One of the members of my assigned father's church told me that she had made several attempts to get my assigned father to fill out the FAFSA form in order for me to get financial aid and possibly apply to the University of West Georgia, where her daughter attended. However, he neglected to do so. I didn't understand how a man who was so well educated didn't want to see his assigned child educated in the same fashion.

I used to wonder why I was treated indifferently, and it dawned on me that I was not a part of these people in a biological sense. My skin color was different, my hair texture was different, my body was different—my everything was just different from them.

Looking back on these historical moments that have taken place in my life, I realize that I am an overcomer. I am more than a conqueror and I have an inner strength that was formed from the trials and tribulations of my life.

Do you know the process of how a pearl becomes a pearl? Pearls are formed when an irritant, such as food, a grain of sand, or even a piece of the mollusk's mantle becomes trapped in the mollusk. To protect itself, the mollusk secretes substances that it also uses to build its shell—aragonite (a mineral) and conchiolin (a protein). These substances are secreted in layers and a pearl is formed. The sand, food, and mantle are all irritants; however, they are needed to create something valuable and precious. My past was an irritant of sorts; however, I have become a priceless contributor to society. My experiences don't define me; however, they have refined me. I am not without flaws, as my scars have become my beauty marks. Embrace all that you have become. Take a step back and adore the beautiful mosaic that is *you*!

Bask in the presence of your greatness. By the way, the pearl is my birthstone—how fitting.

Day One

The Beginning

Genesis 1:1–4 (NKJV): In the beginning God created the heaven and the earth. And the earth was without form and void; and darkness was upon the face of the deep. And the spirit of God moved upon the face of the waters. And God said, let there be light; and there was light. And God saw the light that it was good; and God divided the light from the darkness.

Two teenagers conceived me, an eighteen-year-old male and a fifteen-year-old female. My birth grandmother tried to have me aborted; however, my birth mother was too far along to have an abortion. My birth grandmother advised people that my birth mother had cancer, because she wanted to avoid the embarrassment of a teen pregnancy. After my delivery, I was left at the hospital and turned over to Westchester County Family and Children's Services.

What are your memories concerning the beginning of your life, e.g., origin of birth, family heritage, etc., or the beginning of a particular challenge? How did you feel about it?

Day Two

The Assignment

Ephesians 1:5 (NIV): In love, He predestined us for adoption to sonship through Jesus Christ, in accordance to His pleasure and will.

A couple that could not conceive was assigned to care for me. My assigned father was a pastor, a Vietnam veteran, and a jack-of-all-trades. He was the first man I ever loved. I thought my assigned dad could do anything! His first wife and I did not have the best relationship, even in my infancy. My assigned father used to jokingly tell me that when I was introduced to them, I leaned in his direction and reached for him. I had the spirit of discernment even back then (smile). I am an empath.

What do you think about your assignment here in the Earth realm? What events led up to your destiny moment? Is your story still being written? What have you learned along the way? Whose life have you touched in a tangible way?

Day Three
The Betrayal

Luke 22:48 (AMP): And Jesus said to him, "Judas, are you betraying the Son of Man with a kiss?"

The first time I learned that I was assigned to this couple and not naturally/biologically conceived by them was on a Sunday after morning worship. One of the children from my assigned dad's church came home with us to have dinner. As we played outside, she advised me emphatically that my "uncle" was really not my uncle. Imagine the shock, betrayal, rejection, fear, and confusion I felt after receiving this news.

Have you ever felt betrayed, abandoned, or lied to? What was your initial reaction to the news, situation, or issue? How did you handle it? Did you use wisdom and prayer or revert to your former self prior to coming into self-realization?

Day Four

The Isolation

Ezekiel 18:4 (AMP): Behold (pay close attention), all souls are Mine; the soul of the father as well as the soul of the son is Mine.

After I learned that I was assigned to this family, I felt different. I initially thought that I had been kidnapped. I asked my assigned parents where my real family was. Why had I been given away? My assigned father, being the pastor he was, responded with the above scripture. He advised me that even though I was assigned, I belonged to God—especially my soul! I was too young to understand the theological reference back then.

Have you ever felt isolated, abandoned, lied to, or been lied on? What were the circumstances? Did you realize that, after all was said and done, you were the son/daughter of ancestral Kings and Queens, and that the betrayal was insignificant compared to the future glory you would experience?

Day Five

The Trials

James 1:2 (NIV): Consider it pure joy, my brothers and sisters; whenever you face trials of many kinds.

I suffered many types of abuse with this assigned family of mine. My assigned mother physically, emotionally, and mentally abused me. I didn't understand why I was ostracized at such a young age. I was chubby and wore pretty-plus sized clothes. I had wide feet and sandy brown hair. I was light-skinned, with a huge beauty mark positioned on the left side of my forehead. I was a misfit in the eyes of my peers. My nickname in junior high was "doughnuts."

Can you recall a time in your life where you were mistreated for no reason? What were the circumstances? How did you feel? What was your solace?

Day Six
The First Suicide Attempt

Romans 8:13 (NIV): For if you live according to the flesh, you will die; but if by the Spirit you put to death the misdeeds of the body, you will live.

My assigned father was a very tall man. He was six feet and three inches. He worked for Lipton Tea at this time. He traveled to different territories throughout New England. As a traveling salesman, he was issued a compact company car. His height made it difficult on his knees and the pain he endured was excruciating. He had to have orthoscopic surgery. I was in junior high school; I was teased for being chubby, amongst other things kids tease you about. I couldn't understand why my home life was so different from my peers. Their parents showed them love beyond measure. My assigned mother was always comparing me to other people. My assigned father was preoccupied with his job, church, motorcycle club, and TV ministry. I felt isolated, alone, and peculiar. I went into my assigned father's armoire and took a handful of his pain medications. I wrote a note, laid down in my bed, and waited for death to happen to me.

Can you recall a time in your life when you wanted to call it quits, throw in the towel, and literally die? What was that moment like? What or who got you through it?

Day Seven

I Don't Eat Watermelon

Ephesians 6:4 (TLB): And now a word to you parents. Don't keep on scolding and nagging your children, making them angry and resentful. Rather, bring them up with the loving discipline the Lord himself approves, with suggestions and godly advice.

I was in Atlanta, Georgia, visiting my assigned grandfather on my assigned mother's side. He was a nice man—he was good to me and he never treated me differently. I was asked by my assigned mother to remove her watermelon rinds from the coffee table and throw them in the trash. I went to retrieve the rinds and was met with a slap! My assigned mother said I had an attitude. I lost it! I grabbed her and pinned her against the wall! I was tired of the abuse. It took her two sisters and another young lady, Portia, to pull me off her. I stayed with her now-deceased sister, Diana, that night. My assigned mother threatened to leave me in DFACS custody, but my assigned father told her to bring me back home.

Have you ever snapped? What brought you to that point? What was the situation? Was there a resolution? Have you considered therapy/counseling?

Day Eight
The Colclough Family

Proverbs 18:24 (MSG): Friends come and friends go, but a true friend sticks by you like family.

The Colclough family started out as members of my assigned father's church on 521 Howard Avenue. They had four children. Their eldest daughter, Marilyn, aka "Mert," was my after-school caregiver. Their middle daughter, Serrena, did my hair and played double Dutch with me. I enjoyed going over there, because they treated me like the baby of the family. When I was having "heated fellowship" at my assigned house, I would run away to their house. I hated going home, and Mert knew it, but what could we do? It was the 80s and the laws were different back then.

Amid everything that you have been through, was there a friend, companion, or loved one that you found to be comforting to you during your trials? Who was it? What role did they play in being a salve for your wound? Are they still a part of your life?

Day Nine

Pastor Julia Mae Brown, aka "Grandma"

Proverbs 31:10 (AMP): An excellent woman [one who is spiritual, capable, intelligent, and virtuous], who is he who can find her? Her value is more precious than jewels and her worth is far above rubies or pearls.

Anyone who knows me knows that I *loved* my assigned grandmother, Pastor Julia Mae Brown, aka Mae! My assigned grandmother was the sweetest, kindest, most spiritual woman I knew. She never treated me differently. I spent every winter break, spring break, summer break, Thanksgiving, and Christmas break with her. When things became unbearable, I ended up living with her during my freshman year and sophomore year of high school. The years I spent with her were so refreshing. She lived the spiritual life she preached about. I learned so much from her during that time. I miss her dearly!

Who imparted wisdom into your life? What did they mean to you? What impact did they have on your life? Are they still living? What have you done for them in return to show your gratitude?

Day Ten

Broccoli, Cheese, and Eggs

Matthew 17:20–21 (KJV): "And Jesus said unto them, Because of your unbelief: for verily I say unto you, if ye have faith as a grain of mustard seed, ye shall say unto this mountain. Remove hence to yonder place; and it shall remove; and nothing shall be impossible unto you. But this kind goeth not without prayer and fasting."

My assigned father was an advocate for fasting and prayer via consecration. I remember one summer we spent the entire summer living in the church on a consecration. We ate broccoli, cheese, and eggs for dinner at six p.m. every evening. During that consecration I saw the prayers of the saints answered on another level. There was one member who had been praying for her spouse to get saved for several years. Her spouse came to church after the consecration. He was dressed to the nines in a blue suit. When the prayer to receive salvation was over, his suit was brown. The spirit fell upon him, and he received salvation. He later became a bishop. Look at God!

Was there a time in your life where you laid before God and he answered you in such a way that blew your mind? What did you pray for? What did you consecrate? Did that event draw you closer to God?

Day Eleven
Cancer

Isaiah 53:5 (AMP): But He was wounded for our transgressions. He was bruised for our guilt and iniquities; the chastisement [needful to obtain] peace and well-being for us was upon Him, and with the stripes [that wounded] Him we are healed and made whole.

My assigned grandmother was diagnosed with breast cancer. She didn't divulge the totality of her illness to all of us until much later in the phase. She was standing on the word of God and using holistic methods of healing. I wish that she had discussed the illness and the methods for dealing with her prognosis, because she possibly could have spent more time with us on this side had she elected to have a mastectomy. She was a jewel to the earth as well as the body of Christ whom I miss dearly.

What illness have you faced that caused you to lean on positive confessions, prayer, and journaling? How did that experience affect you? Did you tell others about your situation, or did you keep it between you and God only?

Day Twelve

Back and Forth

II Thessalonians 2:15 (KJV): Therefore brethren, stand fast, and hold the traditions which ye have been taught, whether by word, or our epistle.

My high school years were turbulent when my assigned grandmother became ill. I started off at one school that I loved, only to be transferred to another school, and another school, and another school, and then back to my "love." When your home life is unstable, it impacts your academics greatly. I had to buckle down and separate the chaos of my home life from my academics. I have always loved school—it was my safe haven. I was a member of the National Honor Society and listed in *Who's Who Among American High School Students.*

Name a time in your life where you had to stand fast and hold on because your very life depended on it. Were you tossed to and fro like a ship without a sail or did you find an anchor? Who or what was your anchor or safe haven?

Day Thirteen

August 9, 1990

2 Kings 2:2 (KJV): And it came to pass, when the Lord would take up Elijah into heaven by a whirlwind, that Elijah went with Elisha from Gilgal.

August 9, 1990, was a pivotal moment in my life. My beloved assigned grandmother took her eternal rest. I was in the room when she passed. I always felt that those of us who were in the room upon her passing were passed a mantle. She was a pastor, a prophetess, a wife, a mother, a grandmother, an aunt, a friend, and a cousin, but more importantly she was anointed and a force to be reckoned with. When she prayed, the atmosphere shifted. She carried a majestic mantle and I believe it was transferred to me as she transitioned from this physical world.

Have you ever lost someone who wore several hats in your life? How did their death impact your life? What steps have you taken to heal the void in your heart?

Day Fourteen

Break It Up!

Exodus 14:14 (AMP): The Lord will fight for you while you [only need to] keep silent and remain calm.

I went to church one Sunday only to be met by chaos—two of my assigned father's sisters came to the church house to beat me up! They alleged that I had stolen sheets and towels from one of them. My assigned dad's first cousin "Gee-Gee" advised her sisters of the allegations, and they blocked my assigned dad's sisters from attacking me, because they knew the allegations were false. Crazy!

Have you ever had a situation where you needed God to fight for you? Who was raised up to be your ally? How did you feel when the event was over? Vindicated? Victorious?

Day Fifteen
Walk This Way

Isaiah 43:20 (GNT): Even the wild animals honor me; jackals and ostriches will praise me when I make rivers flow in the desert to give water to my chosen people.

It was senior year and I was graduating from high school. I was a member of the National Honor Society and listed in *Who's Who Among American High School Students.* I arrived at St. Francis Prep excited to walk the aisle, only to be greeted by Sister Jean Marie, our principal. She informed me that my tuition was past due and that I would be unable to walk the aisle with my peers. I was devastated, to say the least. All my hard work and diligence evaporated like helium in a popped balloon! Sister Rita Haberlack, my tenth-grade literature teacher, went to bat for me. She told the principal that it wasn't my fault that my assigned father was behind on tuition payments. She said, "This young lady worked hard and is a good student; let her walk!"

Has God ever provided for you in such a way that you knew it was Him and nobody else? Has someone ever spoken on your behalf, in your favor? Who was it that watered you in your dry place? Write about that time and how you felt when it took place.

Day Sixteen
Willie B.

II Samuel 13:14 (NIV): But he refused to listen to her, and since he was stronger than she, he raped her.

I was eighteen years old and a virgin. There was a twenty-seven-year-old young man I knew from church. He was blowing kisses at me on the sly and winking at me; it made me uncomfortable and I didn't know whom to tell. He went from small things to busting into the bathroom on me while I was in the shower. It escalated to me being in a towel and him pinning me on the bed and kissing on me. I cried silently. I called a pastor friend of mine and recapped the incidents. They told me to leave ASAP! I called my assigned dad to advise him of the incident, and instead of supporting me, he asked, "What did you do to him?" I was floored! What did I do? I wasn't leading this silverback lookalike from the local zoo on. Really? I was hurt that my assigned dad didn't believe me. I told him most men would have been on the first plane to where I was to knock this primate lookalike out!

Have you ever had a time in your life when you were violated and nobody believed you? How did that make you feel? Did you isolate yourself? Did you seek counseling? Are you still dealing with that issue? What steps are you taking or have you taken to move towards healing?

Day Seventeen
The Ejection Experience

Matthew 8:20 (KJV): And Jesus saith unto him, the foxes have holes, and the birds of the air have nests; but the Son of man hath not where to lay his head.

I was being booted out of New York. I called my friend in Atlanta, Georgia, and told her my situation. Her mother told me to pack up and move in with them. In 1995 I left Queens, New York. I reserved a one-way ticket to Atlanta, Georgia. I boxed up my items and shipped them to East Point, Georgia, then packed my suitcase and said goodbye to the city that never sleeps! I loved New York, but my time there was up! I miss the food, the frankness of the people, the mass transit, and going to the city in the winter—there is no place like New York! I loved New York, but at that time there was no love there for me.

Have you ever had to leave a dry place that you were comfortable with and familiar with, only to go someplace unchartered? How did you feel when going through this transition? Were you alone? Did you have friends/family ushering you through this process?

Day Eighteen

Welcome to Atlanta

Isaiah 43:19 (TLB): For I'm going to do a brand-new thing. See, I have already begun! Don't you see it? I will make a road through the wilderness of the world for my people to go home and create rivers for them in the desert!

I arrived in Atlanta, Georgia, on June 1, 1995! I was elated to be here. It was my fresh start; my new page in history. I was naïve as to what things I would encounter here, but I was glad to be in a place where the feeling of being unwanted was placed on *pause!*

Have you ever been given a second chance? Have you ever been repositioned? How did you feel in your new place? What was the scenery of this habitation? Who were your new neighbors, friends, and/or associates?

Day Nineteen
Work Ethic

2 Thessalonians 3:10 (AMPC): For while we were yet with you, we gave you this rule and charge: If anyone will not work, neither let him eat.

When I arrived in Atlanta, I was fired up! I wanted to get a job and get familiar with my surroundings. I had dreams of finding love and starting a family. I wanted the things that I often dreamed about while watching TV or flipping through a magazine. I wanted the life that I'd seen my friends have while growing up. I ended up working two jobs for about six months. I was determined to be successful!

Did you ever have a goal or dream that you wanted to fulfill? What did you do to work at it and birth it into fruition and completion? Are you still working on it? What is stopping you from finishing it?

Day Twenty

Guard Your Heart

Proverbs 4:23–27 (MSG): Keep vigilant; watch over your heart; that's where life starts. Don't talk out of both sides of your mouth; avoid careless banter, white lies, and gossip. Keep your eyes straight ahead; ignore all sideshow distractions. Watch your step, and the road will stretch out smooth before you. Look neither right nor left; leave evil in the dust.

I longed to have a love relationship based on give-and-take. That ride or die type of Mary J. Blige hood love is what I thought I wanted and needed, someone who would hold me down in good or bad times. I got pregnant out of wedlock by a young man whom I loved. Reciprocity was not a tenet of this relationship. Once I advised him that I was pregnant and wouldn't abort or put my child up for adoption, the climate switched from sunny and tropical to frigid, subzero temps. My assigned father told me not to abort my child or give him away, because he was a blessing, anointed, and appointed! I was blessed to become the steward of a wonderful young man whom I love deeply and am honored to call my son!

Have you ever loved and lost? Who? What? When? Where? How did you get over it? Do you believe that love conquers all? If so, why?

Day Twenty-One

Prodigal Daughter

Proverbs 22:6 (KJV): Train up a child in the way he should go: and when he is old, he will not depart from it.

I grew up in the Fire Baptized Holiness Church. I was raised Pentecostal. I went to church twice on Sunday, as well as Tuesday for Bible study), Wednesday for prayer, Friday for revival/council meeting, and Saturday for choir rehearsal. When I became old enough, I fell away from the tenets of my faith, thinking that the world would offer me something better than what I had been taught. What I learned during my prodigal experience is that everything that glitters is not *gold!* The world offered me fool's gold. It wasn't until I was placed in the refiner's fire that I started seeing the gifts that God had placed on the inside of me.

What belief system were you raised with? Did you stray or stay? Why? Write briefly about the circumstances that led you to your spiritual awakening.

Day Twenty-Two
Mission Impossible

Matthew 19:26 (KJV): But Jesus beheld them, and said unto them, with men this is impossible; but with God all things are possible.

I want to encourage everyone in the world to keep going! No matter what the obstacle is that you are facing, you can eat the mountain one bite at a time, or God will level the mountain for you to cross over to the other side. I was always taught that you should go to college and get a degree to move up careerwise. Looking back, I know that to be untrue. I was a single parent who worked a full-time job. I had an infant son, but I still pursued the completion of my education. I was *bold* and brought my child to school with me. I was determined to graduate not once, but twice. I am elated to say that I earned my BS in organizational communication, an eMBA , and a Six Sigma Green Belt certification. I am also a licensed realtor and a licensed insurance agent. I also hold a bartender's certification. That which was arduous and challenging became something beautiful and beloved.

Have you ever been challenged to complete a task that others deemed impossible? What steps did you take to finish the challenge? How did you feel upon completion? Did you celebrate that moment? If not, you should—celebrate *you!*

Day Twenty-Three
Beauty for Ashes

Isaiah 61:3 (NLV): To those who have sorrow in Zion I will give them the oil of joy instead of sorrow in Zion I will give them a crown of beauty instead of ashes. I will give them the oil of joy instead of a spirit of no hope.

I was not the apple of anyone's eye growing up. I was not told that I was pretty, beautiful, or desired—those adjectives were never used to describe me. I was fat and under-loved. I was an overweight, borderline diabetic, high-blood-pressure-having female. I was tired of being unhealthy and always feeling tired. I did some deep soul searching and explored the reason why I always felt ill. My research led to me several doctors who ran extensive tests, and it was discovered that my pancreas was shot! My body was not producing the necessary amount of insulin. God gave me a second chance at life. I work out, eat a healthier diet, and try to exercise more than I did.

Have you ever had a metamorphosis experience? What changed? What were you previously, and what did you become? Did you lose any "friends" during this transformation? Who supported you as you turned into a proverbial butterfly or swan?

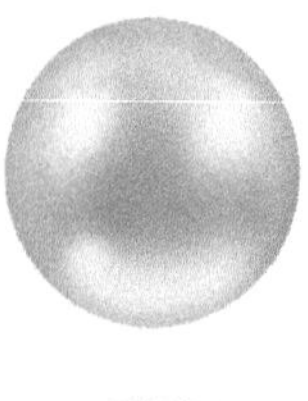

Day Twenty-Four

Hysterectomy

Matthew 7:1 (NIV): Do not judge, or you too will be judged.

People always have something to say, as if their opinion matters in the scheme of things. At the end of the day, God has the last and final say. When I was pregnant with my son, I received so much backlash from church folks, gossipers, and the like. Everyone had an opinion on whether I should keep my baby. My OB/GYN even offered to have her sister adopt my baby. Really? I had someone say to me, "How did you get pregnant with a baby while I am married and cannot get pregnant?" All I know is God is the giver of life, and in his time all things are created and brought into fruition. When he speaks, the earth responds. I had my son when I was twenty-nine. Who knew that eleven years later I would have to have a hysterectomy? God knew. Imagine if I had taken the ill advice of others and aborted my child or given him up for adoption—I would have been childless. I am thankful for my child.

Have you ever been in a situation where others were judging you? How did you feel? What were the circumstances? What was the result of the situation? Did you come out of the experience with greater joy, anointing, fervor, and tenacity?

Day Twenty-Five

Minister Marilyn Colclough Brown

I Peter 3:1–3 (KJV): In like manner, ye wives, be in subjection to your own husbands; that, even if any obey not the word, they may without the word be gained by the behavior of their wives; beholding your chaste behavior coupled with fear.

When you think of the role model of a good wife, whom do you think of? Michelle Obama? Debbie Allen? June Cleaver? Lucille Ball? Florida Evans? Your aunt? Your sister? Your mother? As for me, I think of Minister Marilyn Colclough Brown. She is the epitome of what the Bible would refer to as a "good wife." If I were to select someone to model after, I would select Minister Marilyn Colclough Brown. She is an excellent wife, mother, minister, and entrepreneur. She supports her husband and raises her girls with a firm, loving hand.

Is there someone in your life that you would like to pattern after? Is there something that they do particularly well that you would like to emulate? Who are they? What have they accomplished? Are they available to coach you? Are they aware that you desire to duplicate their success?

Day Twenty-Six

The Department of Corrections

Matthew 25:43–45 (NIV): For I was hungry, and you gave me nothing to eat, I was thirsty, and you gave me nothing to drink, I was a stranger, and you did not invite me in, I needed clothes and you did not clothe me, I was sick and in prison and you did not look after me. They also will answer, Lord, when did we see you hungry or thirsty or a stranger or needing clothes or sick or in prison, and did not help you? He will reply, truly I tell you, whatever you did not do for one of the least of these, you did not do for me.

About nine years ago, I started writing to someone who was incarcerated. Now before you judge me, this individual was somewhat related to me by way of marriage—this was not a love affair of sorts. The Lord laid it upon my heart to reach out to this person despite the circumstances surrounding their case. I have encouraged this individual via scriptures, inspirational quotes, birthday cards, and occasionally adding money to their books for commissary items. The greatest commandment in my book is to *love* one another. Love is an action verb that we must show to one another on a consistent basis.

When was the last time you reached out to someone who was ill, incarcerated, hungry, or in need of clothing? If it has been a long time, I implore you today to find someone who has a need and meet it. How did it make you feel to pour into someone that may not have the capacity to pour back into you? Please continue to pay it forward! We all need *love*—it is the rhythm of life.

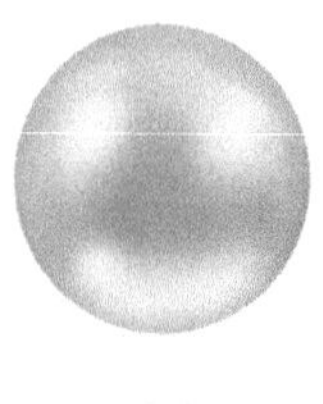

Day Twenty-Seven

Dr. Elder Woodrow Brown

Ephesians 6:10–18 (NIV): The Armor of God
Finally, be strong in the Lord and in his mighty power. Put on the full armor of God, so that you can take your stand against the devil's schemes.

This was one of my assigned Dad's favorite scriptures. My assigned Dad was a pastor, and the FBH Church was *numero uno* in his life. I grew up resentful of his relationship with the church/God, because he spent most of his time surrounded by church events/people. There was no balance, no fun, and no reprieve.

Describe a time in your life where you felt there was an imbalance. What did you do to bring harmony back into the picture? What did you increase or decrease? How did you feel after the adjustment was made? Did you revert to the initial way things had been conducted, or did you stand fast to the conversion?

Day Twenty-Eight

Regrets

Psalm 75:6–7 (Living Bible): For promotion and power come from nowhere on earth, but only from God. He promotes one and deposes another.

I looked at my life and was disappointed—I hadn't accomplished half of what I desired. I didn't have a long-standing career. Being a single parent put a damper on things, because I didn't have the support of the other parent. I had to take jobs based on location and hours rather than my capabilities and education level. I was bummed out, and I felt as though life had passed me by in just a wink of an eye and I had nothing to show for it, other than the fact that I'd survived some horrific encounters. I still believe God can redeem the time and promote me even now.

How do you feel about where you are in life? Have you done everything right by planning for old age and securing yourself financially? Do you rely on self, God, or a mixture of both to supply your needs? Do you believe that God can redeem the time and still make good on his promises even if it looks doubtful? What is your faith, and how do you rest on the promises of God during trying times?

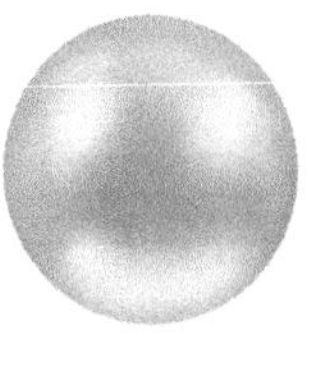

Day Twenty-Nine

Tired

Psalm 73:1–7 (NLT): How good God is to Israel—to those whose hearts are pure. But as for me, I came so close to the edge of the cliff! My feet were slipping, and I was almost gone. For I was envious of the prosperity of the proud and wicked. Yes, all through life their road is smooth! They grow sleek and fat. They aren't always in trouble and plagued with problems like everyone else, so their pride sparkles like a jeweled necklace, and their clothing is woven of cruelty! These fat cats have everything their hearts could ever wish for!

My assigned Dad died; I was the executrix of his estate. Number one, I was in shock that my assigned dad had died, and number two, I was in disbelief at how he had left so many things undone. The job I had at the time had been downsized. I was single and dealing with so many emotions and feelings all alone. My son went to spend the day with his father, and I decided that he would be better off without me. I turned on the gas stove, laid out my $250,000 insurance policy and my will, and laid down in my bed, ready to die. To my surprise, my stove was broken. I thought that was odd, because I had just cooked the day before. The maintenance man came by and said, "This is strange, because your gas line to the stove is operable, but there is a blockage here for some reason." God blocked it!

Can you recall a situation in your life where you were weary, tired, and just wanted to give up? How was the situation rectified? What miracles have been wrought on your behalf?

Day Thirty

Domestic Violence/The Ending

Ruth 2:4–5 (TLB): Boaz arrived from the city while she was there. After exchanging greetings with the reapers, he said to his foreman, "Hey, who's that girl over there?"
Ecclesiastes 7:8: The end of a matter is better than its beginning.

I witnessed domestic violence growing up. My assigned father's sister was in an abusive marriage. I always thought of domestic violence as physical rather than emotional and verbal until I was in the trenches of all three forms myself.

My former spouse was charming and loving in the beginning; however, things changed rather quickly. Instead of my being his everything, I became the opposite.

The night that I decided to end the abusive ride, I was strangled, thrown around, and forbidden to call 911. How had this turned out so wrong so fast? No, it had been brewing, and I'd ignored and excused all the behaviors and signs. The name-calling, the temper tantrums, the excessive drinking, the inconsistency—they all presented themselves. However, I glossed them over. He was a narcissist!

Growing up, I was always told that I would never have the love of a significant other; however, even though I am no longer in this relationship, I do believe that love is an infinite energy that will find me and that someday someone will ask that magic question: "Hey, who's that girl over there?"

Who in your life plays a significant role, and why? How have they loved you in times past and what do they do to display their love towards you? Do you return the love and ensure that they never feel like their loving you is in vain?

Day Thirty-One
Who is your "Jonathan?"

I Samuel 18:1–4 (NIV): After David had finished talking with Saul, Jonathan became one in spirit with David, and he loved him as himself. From that day Saul kept David with him and did not let him return home to his family. And Jonathan made a covenant with David because he loved him as himself. Jonathan took off the robe he was wearing and gave it to David, along with his tunic, and even his sword, his bow, and his belt.

Dynamic duo friendships like Jonathan's and David's are priceless! A friendship such as this is rare. In life, all of us need someone to be our Paraclete, the one who is called alongside to love, care, nurture, and protect us.

I have not found all these qualities in one individual; however, I have noticed that God/the Universe has sent me people along the way to provide what I needed at the time. Sometimes the encounters were unconventional, unplanned, and unscripted. I am thankful for all the people who have poured into me and assisted me in getting to my next level.

Think about the people whom you have crossed paths with throughout your lifetime. What have they added to your life in a positive way? Would the situation have been unbearable without their presence in your life? Contact them and let them know how you appreciate them. Show your gratitude in a tangible way if you can. You never know if they themselves need to be poured back into.

King David from the Bible was often overlooked, undervalued, and belittled by his family. When Samuel came to Jesse of Bethlehem's home to anoint one of his sons to be king, he had seven of Jesse's sons pass before him before the chosen one was selected. Seven is the number of completion. The search was completed, and the new beginning took place when David was selected. Samuel was certain that Eliab was "it" due to his physical attributes. The Lord told Samuel, "Do not consider his appearance or his height, for I have rejected him." The Lord does not look at the things people look at—people look at the outward appearance, but the Lord looks at the heart. David, when brought before Samuel, was glowing with health and had a fine appearance and handsome features. Often, we look at things on the surface based on attraction, feelings, and popularity. It is important for us to dig deeper and evaluate things from a more introspective lens. I am guilty of falling for things based on how they look. However, oftentimes after careful research, I recant the infatuation and make decisions based on my fact check. Let's strive to make prudent decisions that will affect our lives in a positive and impactful way for years to come. It is my sincere prayer and desire that this journal will heal you in the broken places of your life. You are a beautiful mosaic. Be-*you*-tiful!

About the Author

The author has an eMBA and Bachelor's of Science in organizational communication. She also has her real estate license and her life and health insurance license.

The author has an adult child. She loves cooking, baking, going to the shooting range, volunteering with organizations that support those with special needs, and petting any cat or dog she can find.

More than anything, the author finds purpose and meaning in sharing her view of the world and spirituality with as many readers as she's able.

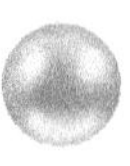

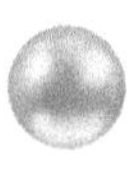

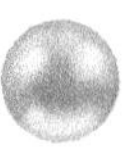

Milton Keynes UK
Ingram Content Group UK Ltd.
UKHW022207120324
439347UK00016B/181/J